LAY DOWN DADDY GAMES

by Jim Manduca III
Illustration by Farisai Makuto
Edited by Nick Iannitti

ISBN-13: 978-1983636332
ISBN-10: 1983636339
Look out for more books by Jim Manduca at www.dadsguideto.com
Lay Down Daddy Games
©2017 Jim Manduca

For Further information, contact
contact@dadsguideto.com

To fathers all over the world.

Table of Contents

9   Introduction

10   Baby Daddy

12   Buried Treasure

14   In-Daddy-apolis

16   Airplane, F-18, Superman

18   Beer Treasure Hunt

20   Blanket Monster

22   Climbing a Cliff

24   The Sleeping Giant

26   Gamer Tag <LD>Daddy (:)|__|

28   It Was the Best of Times, It Was the Worst of Times

30   Gulliver's Travels

32   The LDD Railroad

34   Cloud Watching

36   Hand People

38   The Tickle Claw

40   Human Slide

42   Chin Man

44   Gone Fishing

46   Swimming in the Ocean

48   Pillow Stack Belly Attack

50   Aye Spy

52   Drive Daddy

54   Easy Rider

56   Hit the Slopes

58   Rock Ride

60   Bonus

Introduction

There is something to be said for walking in the door after a long day's work, dumping the shoes, the jacket and the laptop and heading straight for the living room floor to stretch out and decompress. I'm not sure why the floor instead of the couch or even the bed for that matter. Maybe it's because our huge TV — that we overspent on — is there or it's just the empowerment of being able to do whatever the hell we want after having to work for the man all day. Whatever the reason, it's a luxury that usually disappears when we have our kids — but not anymore!

With these 25 easy to follow activities you can keep your kids engaged, having fun and maybe even see less of those dirty looks from the wife when you are taking up the entire floor of the living room. Because now, you're not lying on the floor because you're a deadbeat; you're expanding your child's imagination and spending some quality time with them. By any sense of the word — you are a hero.

So make sure that bathroom door is locked, hit the fan, and enjoy this fantastic collection of ideas I offer to new dads all over the world that I call "Lay Down Daddy Games."

(Don't forget to flush.)

Baby Daddy

You know from experience: taking care
of babies is an absolute blast. Why not
let your own child experience the same
thrill? In this clever spin on dollhouses,
your own child becomes the nurturer,
and your very own home, the dollhouse.

This one couldn't be any easier. Lie on
your back and make cooing sounds.
Ask for a drink and something to eat.
Just remember to let them feed you. My
kids turned our laundry hamper into an
imaginary fridge!

Buried Treasure

Daddy is a treasure! Bury him so the bad pirates don't steal him! Get creative with what they can use to bury you. Try blankets and pillows from the bed, or piles of stuffed animals - remember: you're going to need to do it a couple times with different objects to maintain interest.

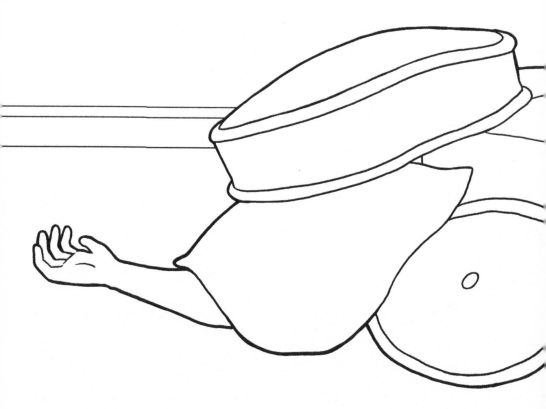

13

In-Daddy-apolis

Remember when we were kids and all we had were some chunks of blue track? Today, all you see are kits with giant plastic sharks, whirlpools and dinosaurs. Don't get me wrong: all this stuff is great, but are the children of today so short on creativity that the toy companies have to do it for them? Good thing Dad's here!

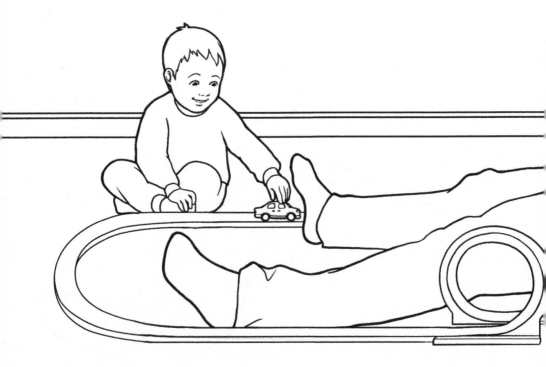

Look up some aerial shots of your favorite race tracks — who am I kidding? Just make it up if you can't remember — and position your body in such a way so when the kids set up their track it resembles a famous speedway. Maybe, while you're at work, you can do a quick search and imagine which ones look the most comfortable. You could really draw this one out and score some serious floor time by switching it up every couple minutes.

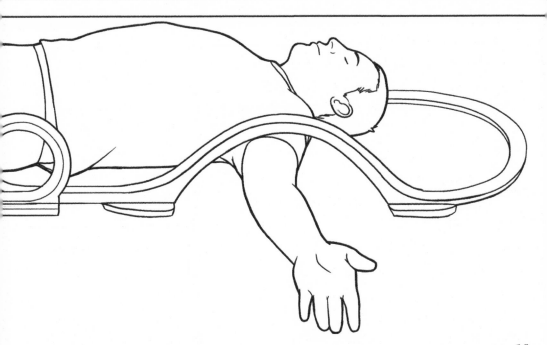

Airplane, F-18, Superman

At a very young age, we begin to imagine what it would be like to fly — either as a bird, an airplane or a person with superpowers. Set your child's mind free and take them to the clouds with this old time fav!

There are three variations of this activity; all of them include lying flat on your back and keeping your feet flat on the floor — this causes your knees to be bent up toward the ceiling and together. Now, ask your child to stand at your feet and lean in onto your shins. At this point, reach up and take your child's arms and slowly raise your feet until they are the same distance from the floor as your knees. You should now have your child suspended from the floor in a horizontal position, lying on their belly. Now, you are ready to fly!

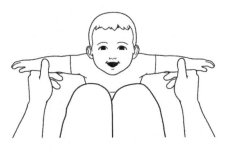

The Airplane! Hold your child's arms out to the side at 90 degree angles from their body. Make the sounds of an airplane "neeeooooowww" as it banks from side to side and you rock back and forth on the spine of your back.

The F18! This time hold your child's arm at only a 45-degree angle making a much more streamlined design. Make your banks much quicker and make more of a "Ssshhhheeeeeeewww" sound to imitate the sound of a jet engine!

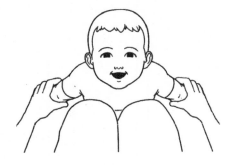

Superman! This is a personal favorite. Hold your child's arms straight up in line with their body and instead of making any sound effects, sing the Christopher Reeve-era Superman theme with "da da daaah! dah-dah-da-da-daahh..!" If you have trouble remembering the slower/gentler part, feel free to slip into the similar section from the Star Wars theme before returning to the "da da dah's."

Beer Treasure Hunt

How are things going so far? A treasure trove of ideas, isn't it? Let's take this next one a step farther.

You're thirsty... but the fridge is over there. Luckily, you've got an intrepid explorer on your hands, just waiting for a mission — sounds like treasure hunt time!

How this works is simple: speak in a pirate's voice (accent training not included) to really sell it and get your child excited. Start with something less conspicuous to the spying eyes of Mommy: let's say your daughter's name is Becky, "Pirate Becky, explore the ship and find me some treasure that is soft and usually found in a bedroom — aaarrrr!". Watch your child happily run off in search of a pillow — get the idea? Sprinkle a few other items throughout the game, but make sure you ask for the remote and a beer from the fridge early — before your child loses interest and goes off to play with her toys, happy to have played with Dad.

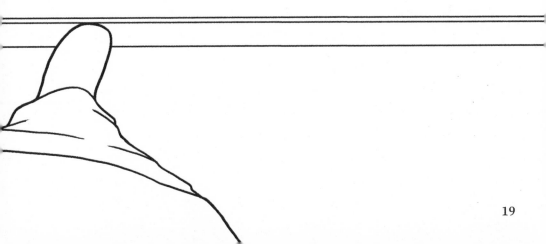

Blanket Monster

This one is a lot of fun, and gives you a chance to lie silently for even just a few sweet moments. There's something hiding in the murky depths, but what is it? And, more importantly, when will it strike? Hopefully no lost child wanders too close... Be creative with the color blanket you are using. Green? You could be a swamp monster. Black? Why not a tar pit? Have fun with it, but be careful: Your child may want to attack you while you are not looking so watch those knees to the nose!

Climbing a Cliff

Climbing stuff is fun but it can take considerable effort — so try this. Have you ever seen that in-camera effect where someone looks like they're lying in bed, but another shot shows the bed was against the wall and they were standing the whole time? It's just a trick on perspective — this is the same idea. Climb across the floor using furniture and cushions as foot-holds, just imagine the floor surface is a vertical 90-degree angle from the ground and you are thousands of feet up on a frozen waterfall, a mountain cliff under the water, or a giant's back; really let your imagination go!

The Sleeping Giant

My hometown, the Canadian city of Thunder Bay, not only has a cool name, it has something else that's pretty cool: the Sleeping Giant. It's a huge peninsula resembling the shape of the original Lay Down Daddy. Hop on Google and check it out.

So, not too much to this one. Lie flat on your back and allow your children to drive around with cars or walk around with their dolls. Be sure to cause the odd earthquake once in a while with a big stretch and a yawn. Remember to really play it up!

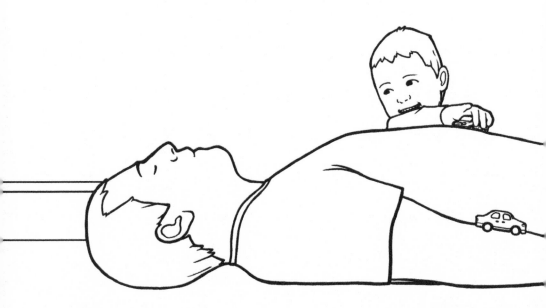

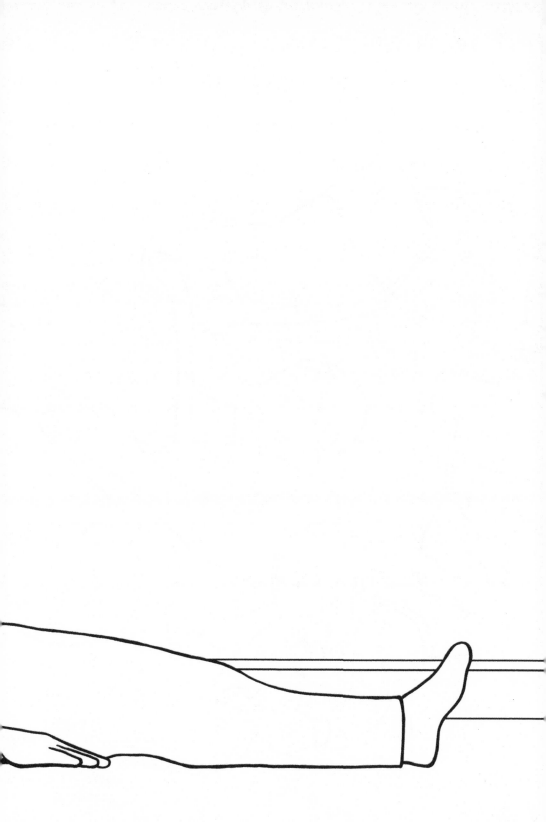

Gamer Tag
<LD>Daddy (:)|___|

Got this one from a friend of mine. Want to play some *Call of Duty* but your kids won't leave you alone? Give them a broken or unplugged controller and let them think they are playing by telling them "Good job! Nice shot!" Easy as that!

It Was the Best of Times, It Was the Worst of Times

The kids just love this for some reason, and it's really fun. Lying face down, cover your face with your hands and begin to sob loudly. Keep your fingers apart just enough to keep an eye on your curious spectator. When they start to move closer or are just about to reach out and console you with a gentle touch, suddenly look up and burst out laughing. This game relies on surprise, so be sure to really startle them!

Bonus: Also seems to work surprisingly well on dogs.

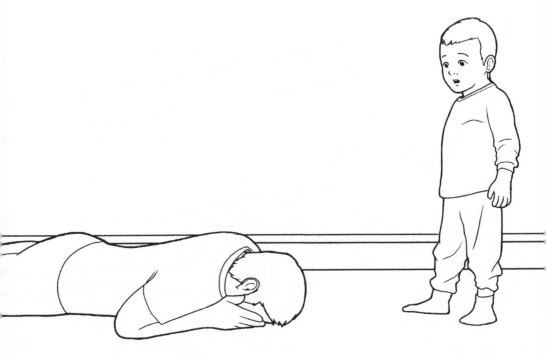

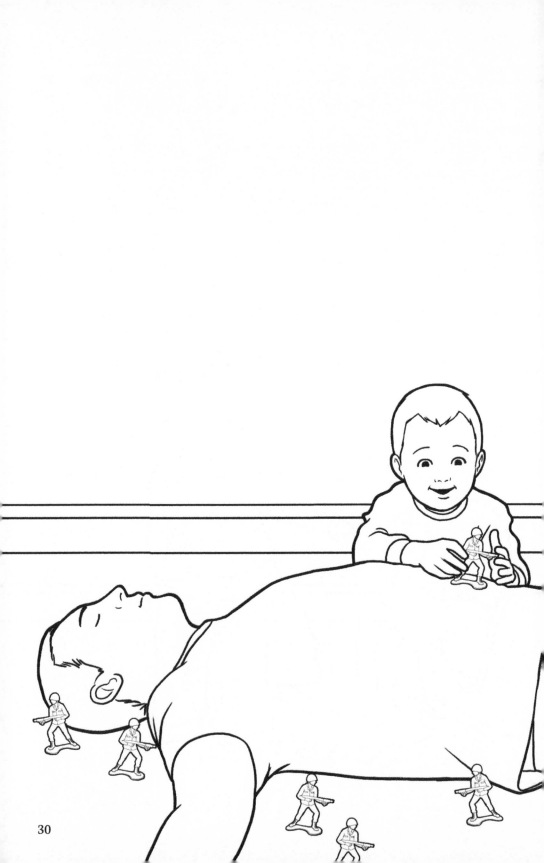

Gulliver's Travels

You've seen at least one of the movies, but probably haven't read the whole book. It doesn't matter, with the power of kids, you can now live it.

Get your little ones to gather their action figures and use them as the Lilliputians (yes, that's what the little people were called — I looked it up.) Maybe spend some time lying down on the couch with the kids and watching one of the films to get them revved up. The 2010 version starring Jack Black seems like it would do nicely.

Side note: If your child decides to tie you down with some string, be sure not to let them run a line across your face under your nose. They can hold you down like that, believe it or not!

The LDD Railroad

This one is very similar to In-Daddy-apolis. Lie down in such a way that you can create some interesting terrain for your kids to build a train track on and around. Get your knees off the ground for a tunnel, and have them build a bridge over your extended arm. Be creative!

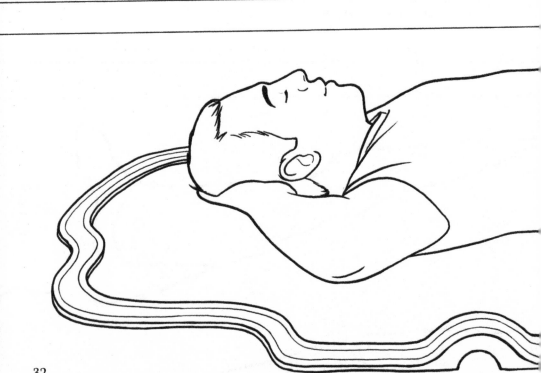

Cloud Watching

Depending on your climate (or energy level), walking to the park is not always an attractive proposition. Here's where a little imagination can result in some really great quality time. Lie flat on your back with your child lying beside you and, in a whisper, say, "Ooooh wooow... look at all the beautiful clouds," encouraging your children to play along. Soon enough, they will be spotting birds, helicopters, and airplanes. When they do mention what they see, ask them things like, "What color is it?" The kids really love it. Even better, if you keep your voice to a whisper, it makes for a really nice, gentle moment — which is great for hangovers!

Hand People

So there you are on the floor and your
child is asking to play dolls or action
figures. You look around and you see all
the toys have been put away. Now, before
you even think of standing up to go get
some toys and messing the place up again,
and even worse, getting up, be creative
and start acting out a story with your hand
using your fingers as legs. Your child will
probably look at you like you're crazy
but just keep going and start asking your
child's hands some questions. "Hi Mr.
Fingers! How are you doing?" Just keep
going. They'll start to play along and you
guys will have a blast.

The Tickle Claw

This is hands down my absolute favorite (no pun intended.) My dad used to do this with my sister and me when we were in our early twenties... er, I mean, it is probably one of my earliest memories.

Lie down beside your child and hold your hand up in the air and bend your fingers to make a scary looking claw monster. Imagine the claw monster's eyes were on the palm of your hand. Sporadically twist your hand back and forth as if it is turning its head looking for its next victim. When your child starts giggling, have the claw monster notice their feet first and then act like it slowly discovers their feet are attached to the their legs and their legs to their body etc. When the claw finally "makes eye contact" have your hand tremble with anticipation and rush in for the tickle. Your child will scream with laughter and it is a lot of fun, giving some character to the Tickle Claw.

Human Slide

Unfortunately, you have to sit up a bit for this one, making it a little uncomfortable. But, hey, you'd do anything for your kids — even sit at a 45-degree angle for a while. Sit on the floor with your back against the couch and just let your kids climb over your head and slide down your chest and belly. You might have to use a pillow or two to lean against to get the angle just right. I've acquired a bit of a belly since the kids were born, so I can almost sit up straight and have a good slide shape. Bonus, I guess?

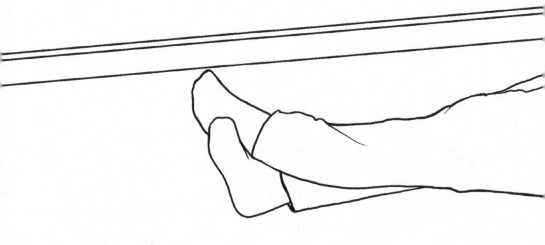

Chin Man

Remember doing this as a kid?
Use some googly eyes or some
washable marker (or permanent,
if you're really badass) and get
creative on your chin. Lie on
your back on the couch and let
your head hang over the edge
so it's upside down. If you want
to enhance the effect, pull your
T-shirt up over your head but
leave the collar just below your
nose. This will cover the rest of
your face, isolating "Chin Man" a
bit better. Have fun with this one
and borrow from some of your
favorite movies: "you lookin'
at me? I don't see anyone else
here..."

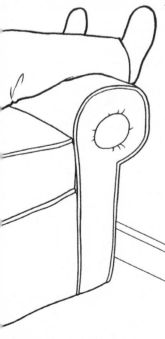

Gone Fishing

Fishing's great, but who has the time or equipment ready to go on a Wednesday evening? I've got you covered (literally) in this next one. Hide under a blanket (preferably blue to act as the lake), and make sure you have an ample supply of stuffed animals or any other toys you have kicking around. Have your child cast a makeshift fishing rod over the arm of the couch onto the floor. I think you know the rest: When the line comes down, pull the line under the blanket. Figure out some way to hook the toy on, then tug the line a bit to give your child a good fight before they reel it in. Boom — dinner is served!

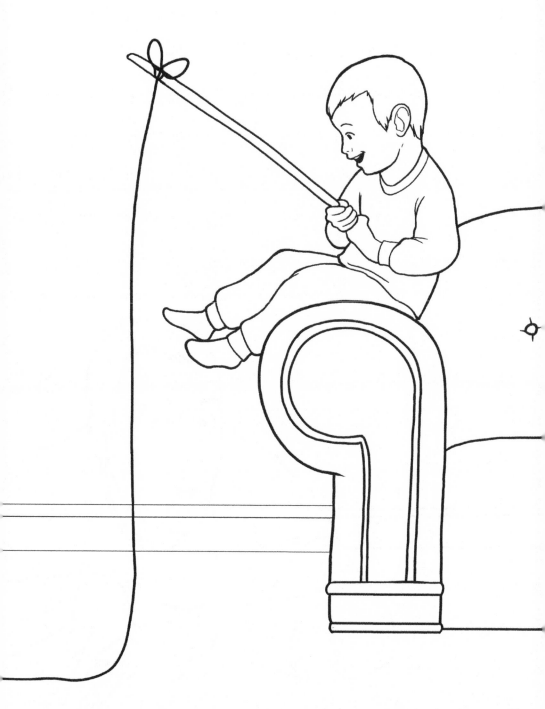

Swimming in the Ocean

Like the cloud watching activity, this one is great for imagination play. Lie on your belly with your children and make huge breast strokes. Gaze at all the colorful fish and the many other sea creatures you see. Again, ask your children how many, what color, and other things like that to get their imaginations going. Wait, is that a stingray? Remember: the more engaged you are, the more engaged they will be and the longer you can keep up the ruse!

Pillow Stack
Belly Attack

This is a variation on a very popular game where you build a stack of blocks and start removing one at a time until it all comes crumbling down. Major difference here is we are adding instead of removing pieces and the pieces are comfy pillows!

Have your children place pillows on your belly one at a time to build the highest stack they can. After a random amount of time, do a belly pump (suck in and then push out really fast) — oops the tower fell and they have to start over! Add a funny sound effect to elicit extra squeals of joy. Advanced mode: lie on your side, your stomach, or in a position of your own creation.

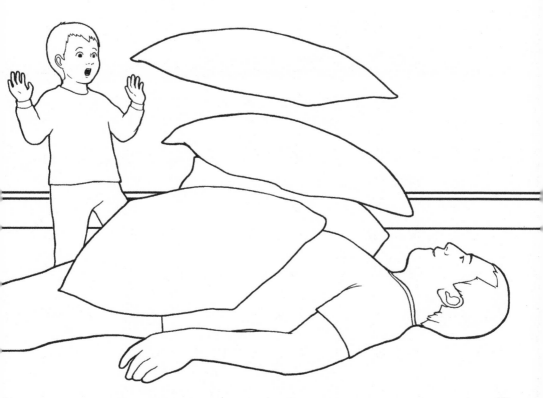

Aye Spy

You just got home from
work, kicked off the shoes,
hung the jacket on the
banister or doorknob and
are now heading for the
living room floor. You get
on your back, close your
eyes, only to open them to
your child standing above

your face staring down at you smiling with anticipation — now what? How about a fun take on "Eye-Spy"!?

Quickly look around the room and find something your child could spot easily just to get things going. Just remember to put a twist on it to make it even more fun. My son likes pirates, so I may say something like "Aar! Find me something shiny and I'll spare ya a walk on the plank!"

Drive Daddy

Vroom! Get it in gear and take to the road with the Dad-mobile! This one's nice and easy. Lie on your back and clasp your hands together with your elbows out making a steering wheel with your arms. Have your kid get in the driver's seat by sitting on your chest and grabbing the wheel. Turn the ignition, pop the clutch and you're off! Convince your child to make some big turns at high speed, and really help sell it by making various vehicle noises and rocking back and forth in the turns.

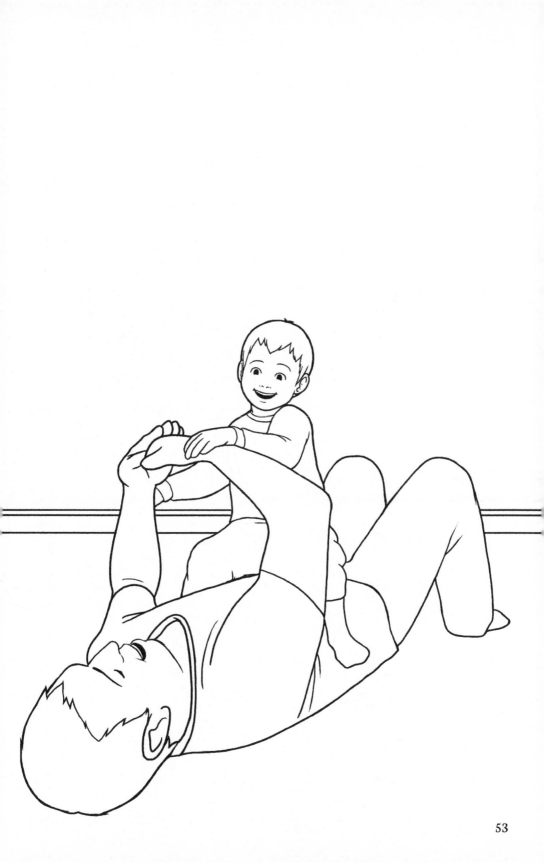

Easy Rider

Get your motors running and head out on the highway! Just like the last one, have your child sit on your belly but try to put your elbows together (just get them close) and stick your thumbs out to resemble some handle bars. After that, just choose your ride and pick the sound effect. A nasally "weeeee" for a crotch rocket and gurgly "gwwwaaaa" for a cruiser!

Hit the Slopes

Take your kids skiing! Lie flat on your back and hold your arms straight up in the air. Coax your child to stand on your belly and hold onto your hands like they would ski poles. Suck your stomach in and push it out to simulate the moguls. If you are feeling really energetic, use your feet to lift your butt off the ground for those really steep parts!

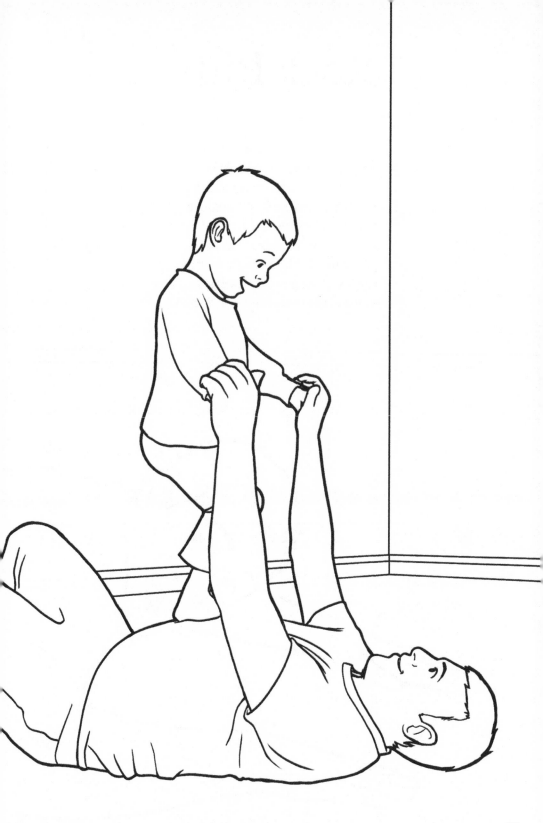

Rock Ride

Yes, this does work. Lie motionless
on your stomach and have your
child sit on your back for a rock
ride! Of course rocks don't move
so just make some exciting sounds
like, "Whoa! Look out! Here we
go!" Your child will laugh, getting
the joke. The more enthusiastic
you are, the more they will enjoy it.

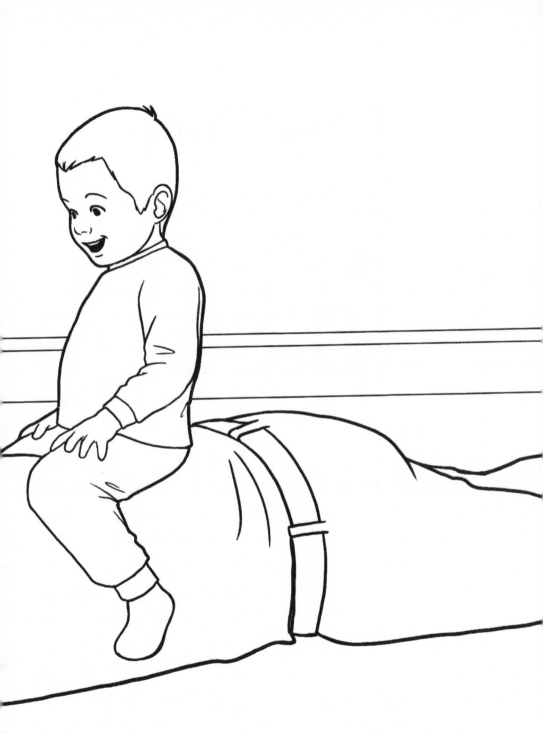

Bonus Game

Whoa! Hold on! We can't let you go yet. Hell, you've made it to the end of the book! For your efforts, you've earned one more Lay Down Daddy game. It's the least we can do!

This one is great if you are engaged in some other form of play with your child and now, well, it's time for Daddy to lie down for a bit. Whatever you are doing, just stop,

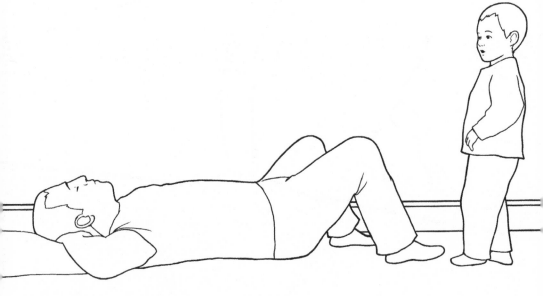

lie down and begin to snore. When your child realizes you have fallen asleep and walks over to assess, awaken from your slumber with a loud roar and reach out for them. Your child will laugh from the excitement and you can drift back off to sleep, ready to pounce again.

About the Author

Jim Manduca is your average, hard-working, well-travelled, chopper-riding, music-writing dad. Like most dads, he'd find himself coming home in the evening after long hours trying to balance his love for his kids with his need for a good lie-down in the living room.

After a few too many quips from his wife about his "lying around and taking up space on the floor", he defiantly devised these games to lovingly engage the kids while still having his precious horizontal time.

This book is written from the heart from Jim to other fathers around the world.

Made in the USA
Monee, IL
18 December 2020